TEACHER GUIDE FOR THE SK̲'AD'A STORIES

Intergenerational Learning and Storytelling in the Classroom

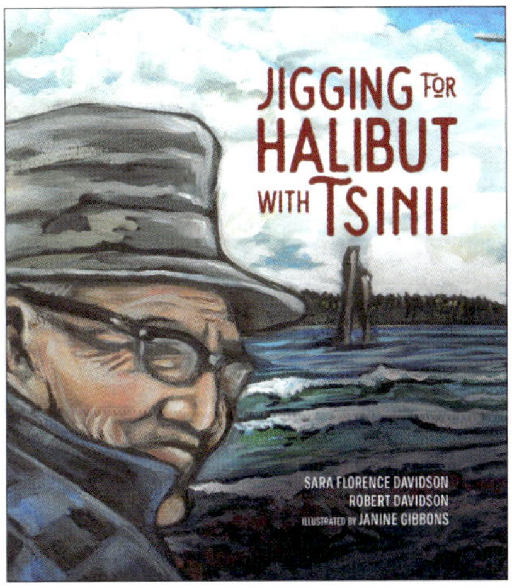

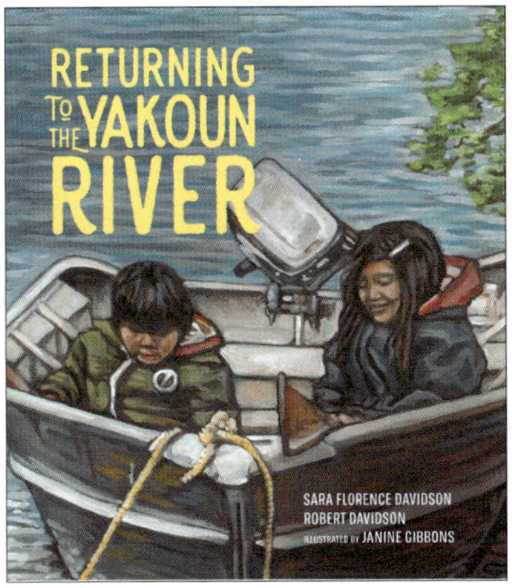

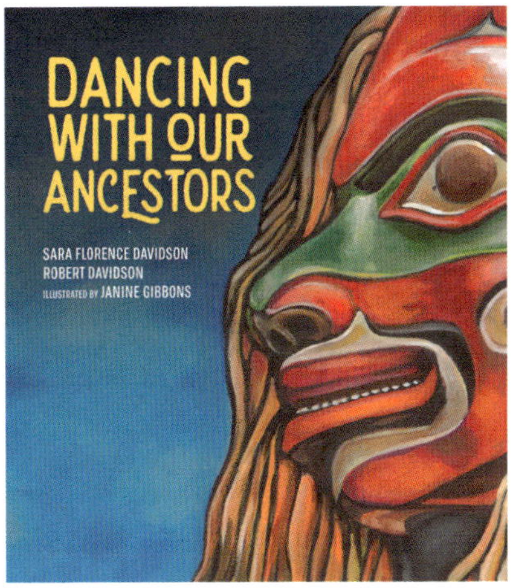

Katya Adamov Ferguson | Sara Florence Davidson

ISBN: 978-1-77492-047-3

Portage & Main Press gratefully acknowledges the financial support of the Province of Manitoba through the Department of Sport, Culture and Heritage and the Manitoba Book Publishing Tax Credit, and the Government of Canada through the Canada Book Fund (CBF) for our publishing activities.

Printed in Canada by Rapido Books
Design by Jennifer Lum
Cover art by Janine Gibbons
Map by John Broadband

Also issued in electronic format: ISBN 978-1-77492-990-0 (PDF)

25 24 23 22 1 2 3 4 5

PORTAGE & MAIN PRESS
www.portageandmainpress.com

Winnipeg, Manitoba
Treaty 1 Territory and homeland of the Métis Nation

CONTENTS

INTRODUCTION

ABOUT THE SK̲’AD’A STORIES SERIES

In the Sk̲’ad’a Stories series, Sara Florence Davidson and her father, Robert Davidson, share family-learning stories from both their childhoods that have been passed down through multiple generations. Through stories from various stages of both their lives, Robert and Sara share how generational knowledge is passed on.

The Sk̲’ad’a Stories series has four books.

Jigging for Halibut With Tsinii (fall 2021)
Learning to Carve Argillite (fall 2021)
Returning to the Yakoun River (fall 2022)
Dancing With Our Ancestors (fall 2022)

The picture books in the series are currently referred to in order of their publication; however, they can be read in any order. When reading them in the order listed above, readers can learn from Robert Davidson’s progression—from learning from his tsinii (grandfather) to eventually becoming a grandfather and sharing knowledge with his children and grandchildren. Each book can stand alone, but readers will experience the significance of intergenerational stories when reading them as a series.

ABOUT THIS GUIDE

This guide is intended to support educators who are reading the Sk̲’ad’a Stories with any grade level and who want to engage in deeper meaning-making within their learning communities. The guide includes three parts.

Part 1: **Teacher Preparation: Understanding Cultural Contexts and the Emergence of Sk̲'ad'a** includes

- Important background information about the culture and knowledges of the Haida Nation
- Introductory information about the Sk̲'ad'a principles and how the stories emerged
- Information about preparing to engage with the Sk̲'ad'a Stories by what Jo-ann Archibald calls "becoming story-ready"

Part 2: **Teacher Learning: Sk̲'ad'a for Educators** focuses on how to use the Sk̲'ad'a principles in the classroom. This section explains

- The significance of the series, and the value of intergenerational storytelling
- Sk̲'ad'a for educators and professional learning communities
- The Sk̲'ad'a principles in greater depth

Part 3: **Teacher Practice: Ideas for Engaging With the Sk̲'ad'a Stories** offers specific suggestions for engaging students with the Sk̲'ad'a Stories and includes

- A chart of themes and connections (for educators wanting to find common links across the story series)
- A list of teaching approaches and ideas for engagement (for educators wanting hands-on activities that embed the Sk̲'ad'a principles)
- A visual sampling of Sk̲'ad'a activity ideas (to help educators choose extension activities that embed Sk̲'ad'a principles)
- A list of the Sk̲'ad'a principles within each story (to help educators dig deeper into the printed and visual texts)

Throughout the guide, find "Inquiry With Students" prompts. These questions encourage further investigation with readers to enrich their background knowledge and understanding of underlying topics and big questions.

In Part 3, look for "Voice of the Illustrator" to learn about Haida visual artist Janine Gibbons and her process and insights for illustrating the Sk̲'ad'a Stories.

1

TEACHER PREPARATION

Understanding Cultural Contexts and the Emergence of Sk̲'ad'a

HAIDA CULTURE AND KNOWLEDGES

I grew up in the Lower Mainland about an hour away from Vancouver, but I regularly returned to Haida Gwaii as a child to visit with my father's family and to engage in cultural and land-based activities. Though our parents were separated, it was important to them that my brother and I maintain strong connections with our Haida ancestry. My early experiences on Haida Gwaii directly impacted my approach to writing these stories and determining which stories would be shared. —**SFD**

The stories in the Sk̲'ad'a Stories series are specific to the traditional territory of the Haida Nation. The map in Figure 1 illustrates where these stories and knowledges are from and shows the lands and waters that brought these stories to life.

  ISBN: 978-1-77492-047-3

Figure 1. Map of Haida Gwaii

INQUIRY WITH STUDENTS: As a class, take a virtual trip to Haida Gwaii on Google Maps or with another maps app to get a better sense of place. Ask students: What do you notice? What do you wonder?

HAIDA GWAII

The islands of the Haida are called Haida Gwaii or "Islands of the People" (Williams-Davidson, 2017). Haida Gwaii is unceded territory, meaning that the land was "not ceded or surrendered through a treaty or other agreement" (Terri-Lynn Williams-Davidson, personal communication, September 19, 2021). The traditional Haida territory includes "parts of southern Alaska, the archipelago of Haida Gwaii and its surrounding waters," and Haida peoples have occupied these territories since time immemorial (Council of Haida Nation, 2021). According to the BC Geographical Names website (British Columbia, 2021), the archipelago was named the Queen Charlotte Islands in 1787 by George Dixon, a British naval officer and fur-trader. This name was considered "official" for hundreds of years: it was placed on Canadian maps and taught in schools, disregarding the Haida language and original place names. In 2010 the Province of British Columbia and the Haida Nation made an agreement and passed the *Haida Gwaii Reconciliation Act*, which officially restored the name Haida Gwaii (British Columbia, 2021).

When seeking to learn more about Haida Gwaii, be attentive to how Haida territory is described. In some contemporary sources Haida Gwaii is described problematically as *Canada's*:

> Pristine wilderness dotted by ancient village sites [is] so protected that only 12 people at a time are allowed to step ashore—this is Canada's final frontier, a remote archipelago off British Columbia's northernmost coast. (Haiken, 2020, para. 1)

This travel article excerpt falsely portrays Haida Gwaii as untouched land and minimizes the colonial impact that continues to affect Haida communities today. Furthermore, Haida territory also includes the waters that surround Haida Gwaii (Williams-Davidson, 2017); Haiken's statement therefore reinforces inaccurate colonial perceptions that Haida territory refers exclusively to land. Lastly, the statement includes the possessive reference to Haida Gwaii as belonging to Canada, when the islands and Haida peoples predate confederation.

INQUIRY WITH STUDENTS: As a class or in small groups, conduct an inquiry into the impact of language. How are Indigenous peoples and lands described in media or digital spaces? What is the message being conveyed if possessive references are used? Have students review various travel websites or blogs from across Canada and think critically about the language being used to reference land, water, territories, and peoples. If they notice any glaring errors, omissions, or misrepresentations, encourage them to reach out to the creators with suggestions for more respectful and accurate language.

  ISBN: 978-1-77492-047-3

SILENCING THE HAIDA

When working with these stories, ensure Haida narratives are prioritized. According to Haida history,

> the Haida were discovered by Raven or Nang Kilslaas when he was travelling all over the earth. During his travels, he found a cockleshell that was being tossed about in the waves. When he approached the shell to see what it was, he discovered that inside the cockleshell there were many children. (Edenshaw, as cited in Swanton, 1905b, quoted in Davidson & Davidson, 2018, p. 3)

However, history texts may describe Haida Gwaii as being "discovered" by European explorers. Focusing on the European arrival, missionaries, trading efforts, and contact with Europeans as neutral events, or describing them from the European point of view, fails to recognize the harmful impact of these events on the Haida Nation. Diseases brought in with colonial expansion wiped out most of the Haida population. According to the Council of the Haida Nation (2021),

> pre-contact population was in the tens of thousands in several dozen towns dispersed throughout the Islands. During the time of contact [the Haida] population fell to about 600, this was due to introduced disease including measles, typhoid and smallpox.

With the dramatic decline in population, knowledge and stories that had been passed on for generations were lost. The Haida who managed to survive were threatened by numerous genocidal and assimilationist policies. "We Were Once Silenced," a chapter in *Potlatch as Pedagogy: Learning through Ceremony* (also written by Sara Florence Davidson and Robert Davidson; see Resources, page 46) documents the systematic silencing in an attempt to colonize and assimilate Haida peoples. As colonial ideologies took root on Haida Gwaii, Haida existence and local pedagogies were threatened through numerous efforts, including (but not limited to)

- Relocation of Haida peoples (disconnected people's strong relationships with local land/water/places)
- Amalgamation of villages (disrupted social, political, and legal structures)
- Commodification of natural resources (disregarded the holistic and relational aspects of Haida culture and spirituality; disregarded community and Haida governance and management of natural resources)
- Creation of policies that sought to eradicate legal, political, and social structures (disregarded legal traditions and notions of how wealth and history are transferred within community)
- The potlatch prohibition, which outlawed legal traditions (dissolved protocols; outlawed spiritual practices, songs, dances, gatherings, ways of teaching generations; forbade the hiring of legal counsel to fight this prohibition)

  ISBN: 978-1-77492-047-3

Potlatch as Pedagogy provides additional details on historical events, their impact on Haida culture, and the ways Haida peoples and cultures were marginalized and deliberately disregarded.

For generations, the Canadian government actively tried to eradicate Indigenous peoples, their governance, legal traditions, and cultures, which is well documented (e.g., Truth and Reconciliation Commission of Canada; National Inquiry into Missing and Murdered Indigenous Women and Girls; Royal Commission on Aboriginal Peoples). Providing students with concrete historical and contemporary examples—such as Indian Residential Schools, the *Indian Act*, and the potlatch ban—helps them understand the impact of these colonial policies. Note that colonial impact is not situated only in the past and associated with exploration and the arrival of Europeans—it is an ongoing issue and should be addressed as such (Tuck & Gaztambide-Fernández, 2013; TRC, 2015).

INQUIRY WITH STUDENTS: Use an historical lens to view the relationship between the Canadian government and the Haida Nation. How has/does the Canadian government change(d) and challenge(d) Haida life and culture? Look at historical and contemporary sources. Create a timeline of changes and/or challenges.

THRIVING HAIDA COMMUNITIES

The Sk̲'ad'a Stories provide examples of the strong connections between Haida peoples; examples of their cultural, spiritual, and legal knowledges and practices; and examples of the strong connections between Haida peoples and the land and sea. The authors and the illustrator are Haida, so the stories and illustrations provide insider glimpses into Haida life, past and present.

Haida peoples comprise about half the population on Haida Gwaii, but Haida peoples also live on the mainland in Vancouver, Kxeen (Prince Rupert), and all over the world (Council of the Haida Nation, 2021). The four main Haida communities are G̲aw Old Massett on Graham Island on the north end of the archipelago; Skidegate in the south; and Hydaburg and Kasaan on Prince of Wales Island in Alaska. While these are large, active communities, there are also many smaller towns. There are also 100 historical villages that once existed on the islands (Williams-Davidson, 2017).

For more information regarding citizenship, land and marine titles, rights, governance, history, languages, and environmental protections, see the Council of the Haida Nation website (Resources, page 46).

INQUIRY WITH STUDENTS: As a class or small group, design a question on a topic such as history, citizenship, land and marine titles, rights, governance, history, languages, and environmental protections. Then have students review resources provided by the Council of the Haida Nation website (see Resources, page 46) with this question as their guide. Invite students to share their findings with the class and beyond the classroom.

UNDERSTANDING SK̲'AD'A

The Sk̲'ad'a principles emerged from my father's learning stories. As I listened to his stories and then reflected on his stories, themes emerged from them. We first wrote about these in the article "Make Your Mind Strong: My Father's Insights Into Academic Success" (Davidson & Davidson, 2016). At that point, these themes were still emerging, but all the principles were represented informally in the article.

Later, as I spent more time with the principles, I organized them into nine statements about learning based on how my father described his learning experiences. I shared these statements with my father to be sure that they resonated with his understanding of his own learning.

Because the principles are based on my father's stories (not the stories of other Haida people) and I did not consult the Haida Nation, they cannot be considered Haida principles. Therefore, when I named them, I had to think of a name that reflected this. As I reviewed the principles, I realized they were really learning principles, so I named them "Sk̲'ad'a," which is the Haida word for **learn**. *Sk̲'ad'a is also the root word for* **teach**, *which is* **Sk̲'ad'ada** *in Haida. This relationship between the two words reflects my belief that we cannot teach without first learning. It also resonates with my understanding that teaching does not always result in learning; therefore, as educators, we need to make learning (not teaching) our focus.*

The Sk̲'ad'a Stories contain some of the stories my father shared with me to help me understand how he learned. The Sk̲'ad'a principles have not been deliberately embedded in the stories; rather, they were already there. I did my best to capture them in the stories the way they were when my father shared the stories with me.

– ***SFD***

The Sk̲'ad'a Stories are based on real people and events. They demonstrate authentic learning experiences, relationships, and teachings from the Davidson family's experiences, which are connected to Haida territory and teachings. As Sara points out above, the stories were not written to illustrate these principles, but rather the Sk̲'ad'a principles emerged from the stories; they were "already there." This guide highlights the principles embedded in local pedagogies, but as different audiences engage with these stories, new insights and observations will emerge—a process that displays both the beauty and power of story sharing.

  ISBN: 978-1-77492-047-3

Sara makes the distinction between Haida principles and Sk̲'ad'a principles. Be mindful that the Sk̲'ad'a principles came from Robert and Sara's family stories and are not generalizable principles for the Haida Nation. However, the Sk̲'ad'a principles can be considered an example of a local pedagogy, since they emerge from learning stories that take place on Haida territory and are interpreted by Sara and her father, who are of Haida ancestry.

INQUIRY WITH STUDENTS: As a class, discuss teachings and local pedagogies where you live and learn. Are there particular Indigenous learning stories that guide your school or learning community? Ask students: Do you have learning stories within your own family? Can you identify key principles that come from within these stories?

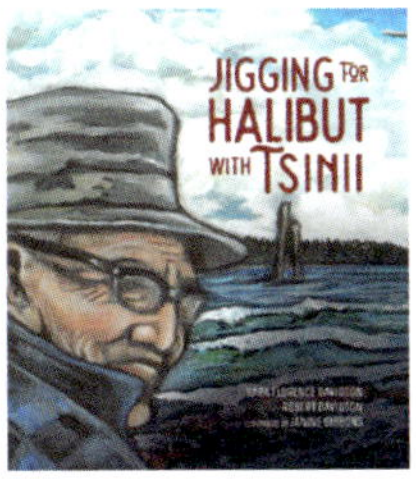

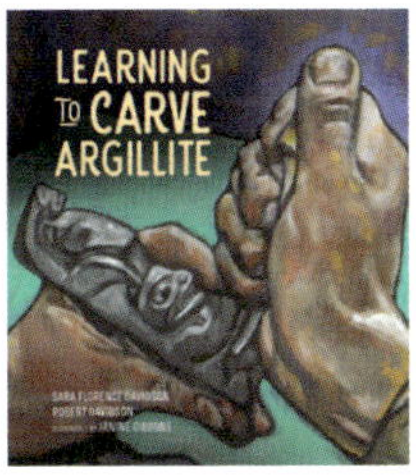

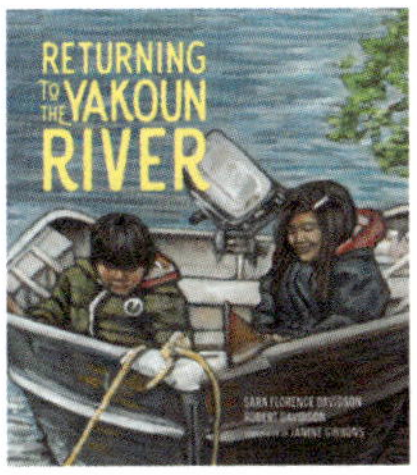

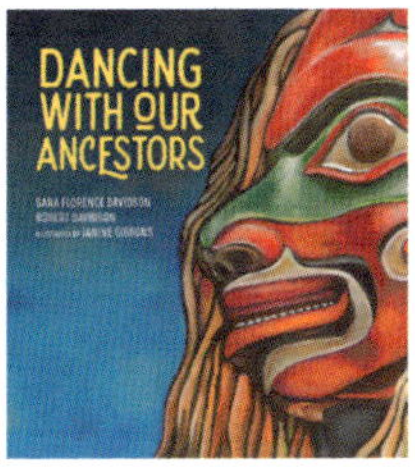

Figure 2. *hlG̲ed sda sG̲waansang* "closely related" or "working together" by Robert Davidson

The central image in Figure 2 is *hlG̲ed sda sG̲waansang* "closely related" or "working together" by Robert Davidson and is found on the cover of *Potlatch as Pedagogy*. In *Potlatch as Pedagogy*, this image is described as a bow and arrow, which represents the way that Sara and her father, Robert, work together and collaborate. Sara states: "When I look at the painting, I see a merging of the past and the present. I see my father as the red foundation—a connection to our past and what is behind us, and I see myself as the blue, being held up by his knowledge" (Davidson & Davidson, 2018, p. 11).

CONVERSATION WITH SARA

The following dialogue between Katya and Sara highlights how Sara collaborated with her father, Robert, to create this series and bring her family's stories to life.

How did you learn the Sk̲'ad'a principles? How are they reflected in the series?

I learned about the Sk̲'ad'a principles by listening to my father's learning stories. When I asked him about his learning, he told me stories from his childhood about learning through a wide range of experiences. As I listened to these stories and reflected on them, I noticed themes. These themes eventually became the Sk̲'ad'a principles.

The stories in this series are either expansions on the stories my father told me or connected to the stories that he told me. The Sk̲'ad'a principles have never been placed in the stories deliberately. Rather, they already existed in the stories.

Could you share some of the unexpected challenges and pathways?

I was amazed at how much knowledge was required to write these short books. For example, in *Jigging for Halibut*, I was constantly texting my father to clarify and learn about minor details, such as the timing of the tides or what material was used to wrap their sandwiches. Luckily, I have memories of being on boats as a child, so I was able to draw from them as well. For the stories to be accurate, there were so many details that needed to be sought from my father. I did not know how little I knew until I sat down to write. I am grateful he was available to respond to my many questions.

I also struggled to fit all the information in the short text in ways that were readable. Sometimes the text would become too fact heavy, and I needed to figure out ways to embed the information without bogging down the story.

How did the idea for the Sk̲'ad'a series emerge?

Initially I was interested in doing the first book, but when I approached HighWater Press with the idea, they requested a series of four books. At first, I did not know what other stories would be included, but eventually I had the idea to share stories from over a longer period. These stories captured my father at various stages of his life. In the first story, he is a grandson; in the second, a son; the third, a father; and in the last book, he is a grandfather. I wanted to demonstrate intergenerational learning from a range of perspectives (books 1 and 2 are written from his perspective, and books 3 and 4 are written from my perspective). I also wanted to capture the sharing of land-based and cultural knowledge. Books 1 and 3 are focused more on connections to the land and water, and books 2 and 4 are focused more on cultural knowledge.

This was important, as my initial thinking about the series was to provide opportunities for educators to become immersed in Indigenous pedagogies while they were sharing the stories with students.

What is the significance of stories for you?

Stories have been such powerful teachers in my own life, I wanted to invite others to learn from stories through this series. I also love that each reader or listener will learn something different from the story based on the knowledge and experiences they are bringing to the text.

> **INQUIRY WITH STUDENTS:** As you engage with these stories, on your own or as a class, come back to these questions: What is the significance of these stories for you? What do you learn from them? Encourage students to begin by reflecting on the questions by themselves. After reading the stories again, consider using these questions to prompt discussion and sharing.

BRANCH OF DAVIDSON FAMILY TREE

The Sk̲’ad’a Stories are about real people and real experiences. An excerpt of the Davidson family tree (Figure 3) illustrates the family relationships in the series. It also highlights the intergenerational learning in these stories—who is learning and who is leading the teaching. Students may want to examine their own family relationships and how stories are passed on within their own families. (See Part 3 for more on engaging with this idea.)

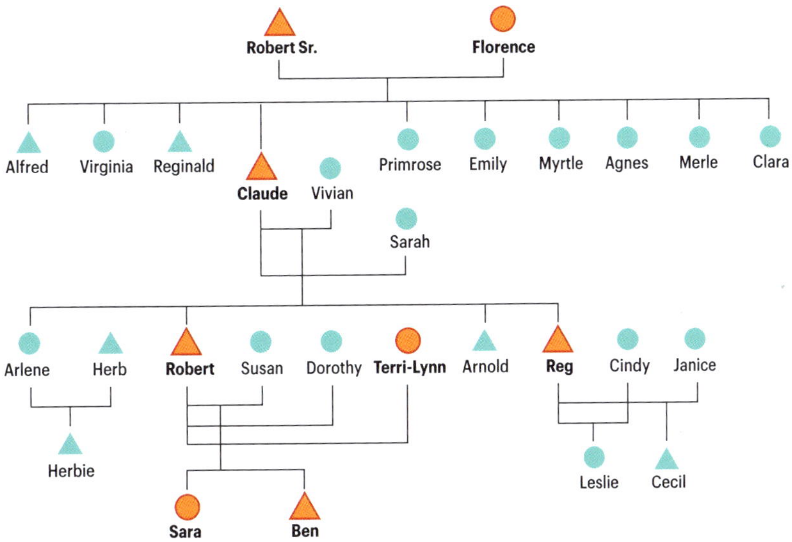

Figure 3. Branch of the Davidson family tree. People in orange appear in the Sk̲’ad’a Stories

  ISBN: 978-1-77492-047-3

INQUIRY WITH STUDENTS: Share the conversation on page 14 with students and invite them to think about the following questions: How can I learn from this process to encourage or support intergenerational storytelling in my community? Encourage students by acknowledging that this is a big inquiry, and suggest they take the first step by asking a family member to tell them a story. Ask another family member from a different generation for their version of the story. Is there something similar that ties these versions together?

BECOMING "STORY-READY"

Although this series is geared towards younger readers, anyone can learn from the stories. Preparing for the work related to stories nurtures personal and professional learning as well. In her book *Indigenous Storywork: Educating the Heart, Mind, Body, and Soul*, Jo-ann Archibald (Q'um Q'um Xiiem) (2008) from the Stó:lō Nation and St'at'imc Nation shares the Indigenous Storywork principles of respect, responsibility, reverence, reciprocity, holism, interrelatedness, and synergy. In her work, she also emphasizes the importance of "becoming story-ready" and being prepared to learn from stories "through the principles of respect, responsibility, reverence, and reciprocity" (Archibald, 2020, p. 24).

Respect: To become story-ready, take time to read the stories on your own before reading them aloud with students. Then, because classrooms are busy places, think about how to give the stories necessary space. Find a time for a read-aloud that allows ample time to read and ask questions and allows students to listen carefully without distraction.

Use the guiding questions associated with the **Sk̲'ad'a Principles** (Figure 5, page 22) to support the deep, respectful listening required to fully engage with and learn from these stories. Review these guiding questions before reading and keep them in mind while reading.

Responsibility: Before reading, prepare yourself for the responsibility of listening or receiving the stories. According to Jo-ann Archibald (2008),

> Patience and trust are essential for preparing to listen to stories. Listening involves more than just using the auditory sense. We must visualize the characters and their actions. We must let our emotions surface. As the Elders say, it is more important to listen with "three ears: two on the sides of our head and the one that is in our heart." (p. 8)

Canadian school systems historically have not valued the practice of listening to these life-experience learning stories. The presence of the Sk̲'ad'a Stories in schools demonstrates a positive shift towards more culturally equitable approaches. Do your best to highlight the significance of these stories as contributions to cultural revitalization and sharing

  ISBN: 978-1-77492-047-3

intergenerational experiences. Help students learn from these family stories in a way that honours both past and present-day Haida culture.

Reverence: This principle "honour[s] the spiritual nature of stories and our individual spirits" (Archibald, 2020, p. 25) and acknowledges the spiritual aspects being reawakened in these stories, such as relationships to places, lands, waters, communities of humans, animals, and spiritual beings. While spiritual aspects may be new entry points for many educators, young learners may intuitively see these connections. Ensure that you are preparing a community of learners willing to consider multiple perspectives, and that you are providing a safe space for wondering, making emotional and spiritual connections, and imagining.

If you choose to engage community members, learn and practise the cultural protocols of your local community or region. Also, if you are sharing learning from these stories with another class or online, ensure that the authors' names and Nation are mentioned and credited. This is more than a courtesy; it is part of storywork. Giving credit to the Davidsons and acknowledging their cultural, land-based connections help to "use the story 'in a good way'" (Archibald, 2020, p. 24).

Reciprocity: Archibald (2020) discusses this principle as relating to giving back and intergenerational learning. Take time to read about how these stories were experienced and shared, and how the learning embedded within the stories is being revitalized by this father-daughter team. In the process of working through their family stories, both Sara and Robert engage in the reciprocal work of storytelling—interpreting, then retelling these learning stories and sharing these stories with new audiences. Story-readiness takes time and is not something accomplished just by reading this guide; it is a longer process and requires commitment to working with and learning from stories.

HOLISTIC ENGAGEMENT WITH STORIES

Jo-ann Archibald (n.d., 2008, 2020) describes the importance of engaging with stories holistically. Drawing on Archibald's work (with permission), Sara teaches about the importance of engaging mentally, physically, emotionally, and spiritually with stories. When Sara works with educators, she invites them to practise engaging holistically with stories using the following framework and guiding questions:

Mental Engagement: Listen to the story being told.

Physical Engagement: Engage in drama activities to make meaning from the story.

Emotional Engagement: Reflect on the story.

- How do our experiences connect with those of the character(s) in the story?
- How might the characters in the story feel?

Spiritual Engagement: Consider the teachings from the story. What does the story teach us?

  ISBN: 978-1-77492-047-3

As an educator searching for curricular connections, be willing to make space for connections between the heart and mind.

> **INQUIRY WITH STUDENTS:** Brainstorm the following questions with students: How might you share your learning from the Sk'ad'a Stories with your local community? Create a class digital presentation where each student or group creates one slide to represent their learning from the stories. Or have students share their own family stories that they were inspired to collect through the reading process.

2

TEACHER LEARNING

Sk̲'ad'a for Educators

SIGNIFICANCE OF THE SERIES

The Sk̲'ad'a Stories are intergenerational stories that emphasize Indigenous pedagogies. Sharing these stories actively preserves Haida culture. And when shared with wider audiences, these family-learning stories inspire more families to share their stories to preserve family knowledge and history.

This series is a contribution to both traditional and contemporary Haida culture. Haida culture should never be portrayed as static and as existing only in the past. **Haida culture is a living culture.**

INTERGENERATIONAL STORIES

Figure 4 illustrates whose perspective the stories are written from, the timeframe and context of each story, and how the stories fit together.

  ISBN: 978-1-77492-047-3

Figure 4. Intergenerational story sharing

INQUIRY WITH STUDENTS: Review the information in Figure 4 with students before reading each book. Ask clarifying questions, such as: Whose perspective is this written from? What else was happening during that time frame for Haida communities? Your local community? Canada?

SK̲'AD'A FOR EDUCATORS AND PROFESSIONAL LEARNING COMMUNITIES

Potlatch as Pedagogy: Learning Through Ceremony by Sara Florence Davidson and Robert Davidson and the documentary *Haida Modern*, available through the Knowledge Network (see Resources, page 46), are useful resources that complement the Sk̲'ad'a Stories series.

Potlatch as Pedagogy provides background and contextual information for a better understanding of the historical and cultural significance of the Sk̲'ad'a Stories. It also supports a deeper understanding of Haida ceremony and protocols, while providing information about the threats to culture imposed by the Canadian government.

Haida Modern focuses on Robert Davidson as artist and activist, but it also shares information that contextualizes the Davidsons' work and provides powerful visual examples and explanations of the artistic process. Use *Haida Modern* to stimulate rich discussions within your professional learning community.

Before bringing the series to your classroom, consider what *you*, as an educator, already know about Haida culture, knowledges, arts, and practices. Everyone has different background information, and it is important to recognize your strengths and limitations as you prepare to guide readers. Think critically about how culture was or is represented or misrepresented in your school experiences.

- Did you learn about Haida culture as a static expression of the past?
- How was the impact of colonization addressed?
- What do you need to know to access these stories?
- As you learn more, think about colonialism on the West Coast of what is now known as North America. How is it similar to or different from colonialism in the region where you live and/or work?

Discuss the Sk̲'ad'a Stories and/or *Potlatch as Pedagogy: Learning Through Ceremony* as a grade group team, with vertical teams of teachers from a variety of grade levels, or within a professional learning community (PLC). These rich texts provide opportunities for deep discussions without the pressures of jargon or long articles. They are ultimately stories about teaching and learning, and therefore offer starting points for discussions. Begin with one or more of the following ideas:

- Think of your own storied lives, personal or professional.
- Brainstorm and journal several stories that have stayed with you. Share these with your colleagues. As you listen to each other, do you find any common elements amongst your stories? What stands out to you?

- Reflect on your stories through the lens of the Sk̲'ad'a principles. Is there a clear connection with one or more principles? Did a colleague help you see your story differently?

SK̲'AD'A PRINCIPLES

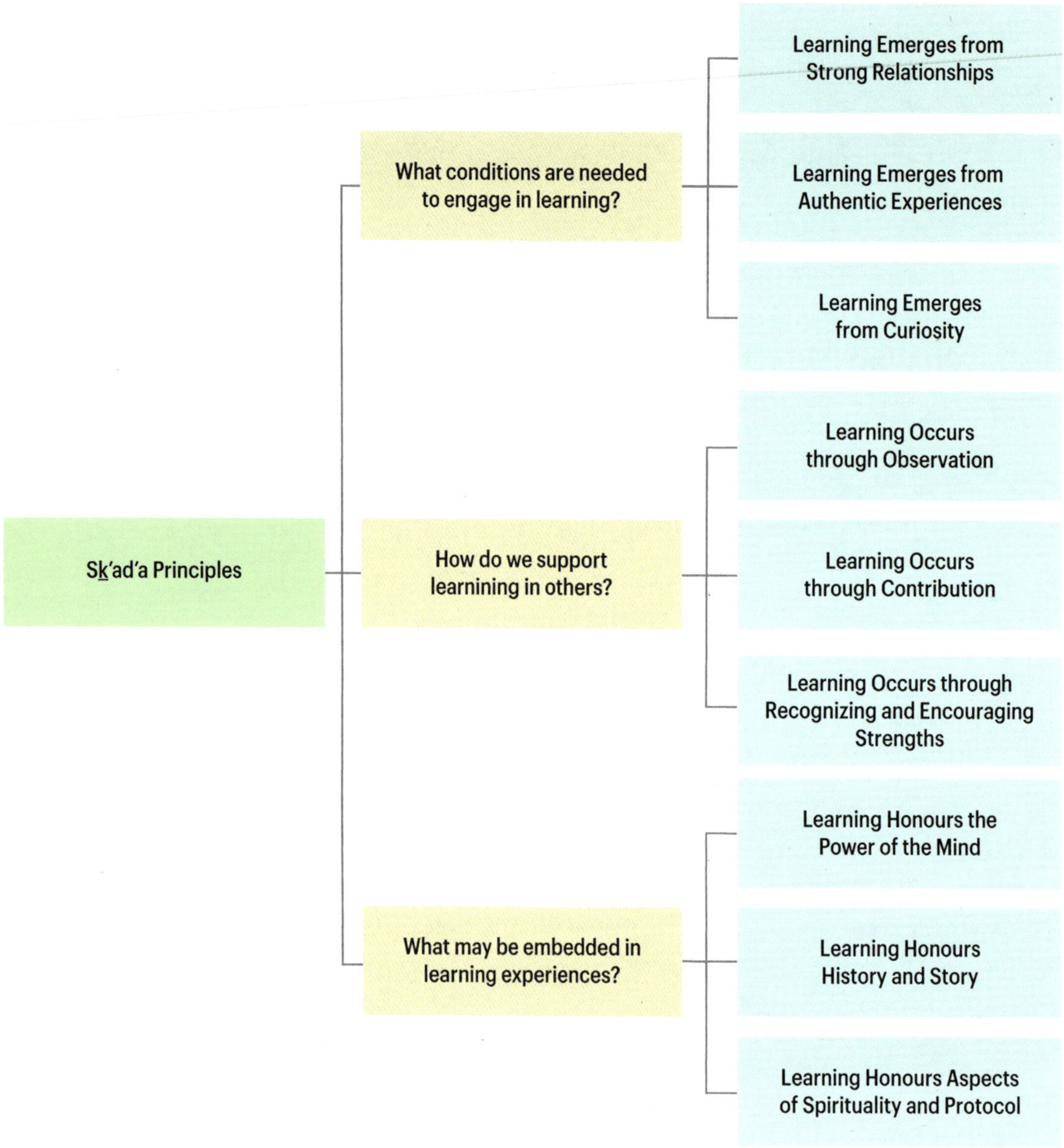

Figure 5. Guiding questions to support learning for others

3

TEACHER PRACTICE

Ideas for Engaging With the Sk̲'ad'a Stories

THERE ARE MANY ways to read and engage with the Sk̲'ad'a Stories. As with traditional oral stories, readers are encouraged to return to the stories many times. The idea of recursive learning is central to Indigenous pedagogies, and this process of returning to the stories can deepen readers' engagement, understandings, and connections.

SK̲'AD'A PRINCIPLES IN PRACTICE: GUIDING QUESTIONS BY SARA FLORENCE DAVIDSON

Use these guiding questions to frame learning contexts and to reflect on your practice.

Relationships

- How can I build and strengthen relationships *with* learners and *between* learners in the classroom or school?
- How can I incorporate intergenerational learning in the classroom or school?

Authentic Experiences

- How can I use authentic experiences to strengthen learner engagement?
- How does the content of my teaching connect with and/or support learners' lives in the classroom and/or school?

  ISBN: 978-1-77492-047-3

Curiosity

- How can I build on the curiosity of the learners in the class or school?
- How can I support and promote increased learner curiosity?

Observation

- How can I include opportunities for learners to learn through observation?
- How can I adjust the timelines in my teaching to accommodate learners who may benefit from learning through observation?

Contribution

- How can my teaching support learners to make meaningful contributions to their families and communities?
- What opportunities can I provide to support all learners to make meaningful contributions to the class and/or school?

Recognizing and Encouraging Strengths

- What do I know about the strengths of the learners?
- How can I recognize and encourage the strengths of the learners through my teaching?

Power of the Mind

- How can I support learners to "make their minds strong" to overcome adversity?
- How can I support learners to visualize the outcome of larger tasks in order to achieve them?

History and Story

- How does my teaching honour local history and/or history that is relevant to the learners?
- How can I respectfully incorporate history and story in my teaching?

Spirituality and Protocol

- How can I honour learners' diverse knowledges and ways of knowing that may include spiritual understandings?
- How can I honour the protocols surrounding Indigenous knowledges that I bring into the classroom or school?

THEMES AND CONNECTIONS ACROSS THE SERIES

Many thematic threads are woven throughout the series. This chart guides connections across books.

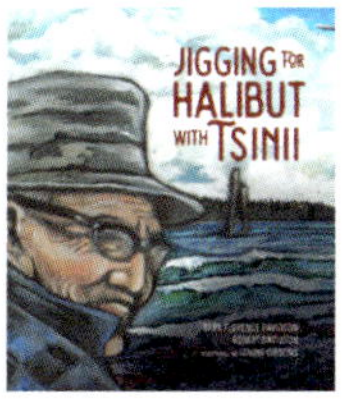

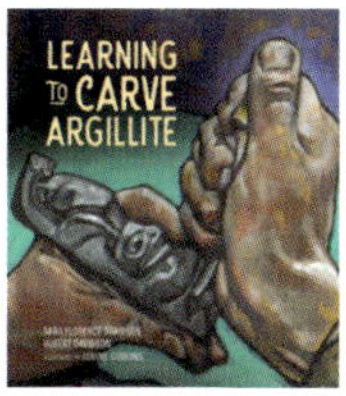

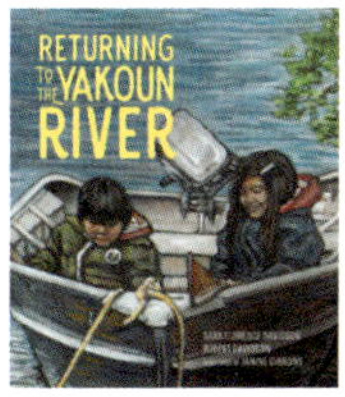

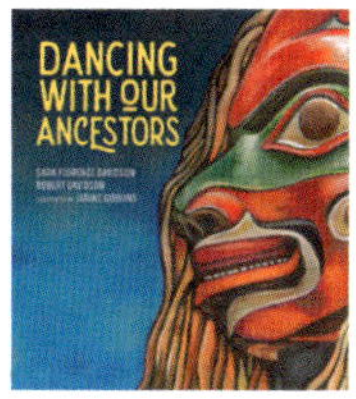

Land and Water	Identify evidence of land-based knowledges (including connections to the water) in each of the stories. • How is land and/or water integral? • How do environmental issues such as overfishing, logging, pipelines, urban development, access to land and water, etc. impact the preservation of stories and of culture? Look for relationships with land, water, animals, and nature. • What rhythms of nature or cycles are present? • How does this influence the stories?
Story	Think about the multi-generational aspects of these stories. Use the Intergenerational Story Sharing chart (Figure 4, page 20) to think about: • Whose story is being told? • What does this story teach? • How does this story teach?
Relationships	Look for evidence of how relationships are nurtured with animals and the supernatural. (For example, talking to the halibut, carving the argillite, becoming the animal in the dance.) Explore themes of adversity throughout and connections to the power of mind.
Teaching/ Learning	Look at how teaching and learning are present in these stories. How does this compare to how you learn in school and/or how you learn best? Look for Sk̲'ad'a principles in each of the stories. Share your own teaching/learning stories.

SHARING THE SK̲'AD'A STORIES WITH STUDENTS

Use the following ideas as starting points for your learning journey. Find connections and extensions unique to your community.

INTERACTIVE READ-ALOUDS

Preparing for intentional interactive read-alouds (NCTE, 21) can help ensure this series connects with other learning or literacy goals you have for students. These stories work well as read-alouds with a variety of audiences. Engage in a back-and-forth dialogue to engage students in deeper meaning-making while reading.

To prepare for an interactive read-aloud, first read the text by yourself. Take notes and keep a sticky-note trail to guide when to pause and what questions to ask. Model reading strategies before, during, and after reading, such as questioning, predicting, inferring, making connections, and summarizing. Meaning-making should be ongoing and organic, and it should occur before, during, and after reading the story.

> **INQUIRY WITH STUDENTS:** Encourage students to make reflective notes to capture their understanding of the story after their initial reading. Return to these stories to see what new insights they uncover. Review notes later to see how their understanding changed. Ask students: What new insights can you uncover? How does your understanding deepen over time?

MAKING MEANING FROM STORIES

The ideas in this section are adapted from "Storyguide: Beginning the Journey," by Eric Gordon and Jo-ann Archibald (1994). Traditional oral stories are often told with no explanation. Listeners are expected to go away and think about the story and any meanings that may surface. Try this with your students so they become familiar with this expectation.

As a learning community, discuss different aspects of the story and share individual understandings. The meaning students make from the story will become deeper as they hear the connections and learning of their peers. Readers/listeners are not expected to understand all of a story or to make meanings in the same way. But with discussion of and active engagement with the story's aspects, understandings may deepen, and listeners may see the story in new ways.

Have fun with the story through role-playing. By putting the movements into action, students experience empathy with characters and situations. Read the book aloud while students re-enact it, listening with their senses and bodies to know the story more deeply and to feel the story come to life.[1]

1 Be respectful of the story while having fun. Imagine that the person, community, or Nation who owns the story is in the room with you and use this to guide your actions. Remember that if we do not treat the story with respect, we will no longer have permission to use it.

MENTOR TEXTS

Use the rich written language of these stories to guide writers in mini lessons to revise, elaborate, and refine their own writing. The narrative flow of these stories does not include a conflict, but rather focuses on specific moments and experiences. The stories can serve as mentor texts (i.e., writing models) for writing personal narratives or family stories.

As you engage in the writing process with students point out how the illustrations add to the story. Discuss how every author and illustrator works through many drafts when bringing stories to written and visual form. Share the in-progress images with students to give a sense of how these books were created and how the author and illustrator collaborated. Invite students to create a story with a friend—one in the role of the author and one the illustrator. The author may use the printed text for inspiration, while the illustrator seeks ideas from the visual images.

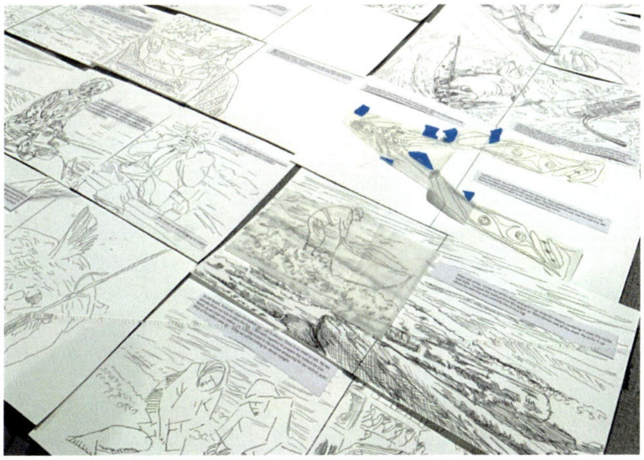

Figure 6. Photo of the writing and illustrating process
Photo from Janine Gibbons, used with permission

Storytelling. What real-life stories do you want to share? Write an **intergenerational story** with a family member or key influence in your life. Begin with a conversation, starting with a question or invitation: Can you tell me a time when you learned something new? Can you tell me a story about when you were little? As a storyteller and listener, work together to retell the story. Come back together as storyteller and listener and discuss the story. How might you write/represent/retell this story? Switch roles and repeat the process.

Explore perspectives. Find a family story and visit the story from several people's perspectives. Retell this story from these various perspectives and explore the learning that emerges from and through the story. How are family histories, cultural traditions, protocols, or spirituality intertwined in this story?

Collaborative storytelling. Find a friend or family member to work with and recall a shared event or experience (such as a recess, field trip, or classroom story). Retell the story using a combination of both of your perspectives. Notice how the experiences may have differed even though it was the same event.

Family Story Maps. Create a family story map (similar to Figure 3) to show how learning is passed through generations in students' own families. When discussing family, open the space for all possibilities and ranges of families. Include found families or heart families for students who live with non-biological parents. Understand that influential mentors, teachers, and friends all contribute to our storied lives. Make an inclusive space where all these possibilities can be honoured. Model an example of this with students.

Image-Based Storytelling. The images in the Sk̲'ad'a Stories are beautiful but are also loaded with significance. Illustrator Janine Gibbons—who is also from the Haida Nation—offers insights that are highlighted throughout this section. Share these insights with students. Focus on how each story is told through the illustrations and visual imagery. Do this with a picture walk before reading the stories aloud to elicit conversations, or after reading to dive deeper into the text.

In the Sk̲'ad'a Stories, Janine uses a combination of big-picture illustrations and close-ups that can lead to discussions about point of view. Encourage readers to write and illustrate their own stories. When students are drawing images to match their own stories, encourage a variety of points of view and perspectives (e.g., close-ups help emphasize important actions).

INQUIRY WITH STUDENTS: How do these illustrations convey Sk̲'ad'a principles? Find one illustration that you think best represents each principle. Look at your writing and matching pictures. Is there one that you want to zoom in and do a close-up of instead?

Janine referenced photographs to create the illustrations, so everyone is recognizable. She used Davidson family photos to ensure the accuracy of the images and to accurately portray the time frame in which the stories took place.

Figure 7. Photo of Tsinii being recreated using digital media in combination with paintings to support the accuracy of the illustrations
Photo from Janine Gibbons, used with permission

Voice of the Illustrator: When Tsinii brings the halibut on the boat, he takes out his new bait and rubs it in the halibut's eyes and says "D'aal ts'ad Kaagaay," telling the halibut in the ocean to bite the bait. Janine Gibbons shares her knowledge of the significance of this action with the bait (usually octopus). A relationship develops between the fish caught and the future catch that represents "sending out a frequency" (J. Gibbons, personal communication, July 6, 2021). Janine explains that there are similarities in the appearance of halibut eyes, magnetic fields, and black holes. She used this visual comparison in her illustrations.

Figure 8. Creating the halibut eye
Photo and artwork from Janine Gibbons, used with permission

INQUIRY WITH STUDENTS: Have students explore science and art connections through research. How do black holes and magnetic fields compare to images of fish eyes? What other connections can you find with animals and nature?

ISBN: 978-1-77492-047-3

CRITICAL LITERACY

The Sk̲'ad'a Stories complement a broader social studies unit that looks at a more complete history of Canada by including hidden or neglected histories of the impact of colonialism and cultural resurgence.

Read the stories alongside historical videos to get a multi-perspective view of a topic or issue. For example, pair *Jigging for Halibut with Tsinii* with a documentary or news story about overfishing.

Numerous resources are available online, but not all are accurate or culturally affirming. As educators, "we must remain informed and continue to review the resources that we bring into our classrooms" (Davidson, 2020). Always preview resources carefully before using them with students. Think critically about how digital media or text will enhance students' learning and engagement with the topic. Remember, just because it's out there does not mean it is fully appropriate.

As a class, watch and review historical footage or videos. Support students in viewing materials through a critical sociological/cultural/historical lens. Encourage them to consider the language and terminology. For example, the video *Haida Carver* (NFB) is a beautiful visual display of co-author and artist Robert Davidson, but the narration has significant issues, such as using the term "Indian," not providing details about the artist, and implying that the art is dying.

Check out "Evaluating Indigenous Education Resources for Classroom Use" in the BC Teachers' Federation *Teacher Magazine* for more specific guidelines on respectful representation and important guiding questions to consider when seeking Indigenous resources (see Resources, page 46).

INQUIRY WITH STUDENTS: As a class, watch the video *Haida Carver* with a critical lens and engage students in rewriting the script to be more culturally respectful.

Involve Families

The relationships between family members are a key aspect of these books. Whatever direction you go with readers, and however you extend the learning from the stories into your school context, consider involving families. Sharing what you are reading and learning about is a great place to start. Circulate the books so students can read them with their families. Involving family and community members in sharing their own learning stories is more complicated, but it creates intergenerational connections that value the voices and stories of families.

  ISBN: 978-1-77492-047-3

ARTIFACTUAL LITERACIES

If you are far away from Haida territory, search digital libraries and online museum collections to find Haida artifacts. There may also be artifacts in your local museum. Pahl and Roswell (2010) state that "every object tells a story."

> **INQUIRY WITH STUDENTS:** Explore Haida culture through artifacts to complement this story series. Ask students: What stories might this specific Haida object tell? What do you want to, or need to, learn more about? What are the issues around Haida cultural artifacts being in museums? Have students look into how Haida artifacts are being repatriated.

Janine reminds us that objects and symbols are alive. Invite students to venture beyond the objectification of an artifact and consider spiritual aspects involved in its creation and its presence beyond the physical/material. For example, Janine gives insights about how the argillite speaks. It holds the power and story of the mountain. The "artifact" is not just an object; it is both historical and alive.

Every visual detail within the Sk̲'ad'a Stories is included thoughtfully and intentionally. Janine drew upon her own knowledge and experiences as a member of the Haida Nation to create the visual texts. Even simple details, like rope, are illustrated by drawing on ancient wisdom.

Voice of the Illustrator: Since I grew up on the ocean and in and around boats, I love knots and have done a lot of paintings of knots, rope (e.g., mooring lines on a boat), and cleats (where you tie off boats on a dock). Stylistically I also looked at mariner societies whose cultures are deeply rooted in the comings and goings of water—so there is a humbleness and simultaneous strength and plethora of ancient wisdom in ropes and knots that I appreciate visually.

Figure 9. Creating the rope and anchor
Photo and artwork from Janine Gibbons, used with permission

SK̲'AD'A ACTIVITY IDEAS

This chart provides an overview of possible activities that connect to the Sk̲'ad'a principles. There is no specific starting point, so select activities based on your students' interests and your learning goals. The Sk̲'ad'a Stories can be read with students from early years to young adults and are even useful for teacher professional development. Choose a meaningful path for your educational context.

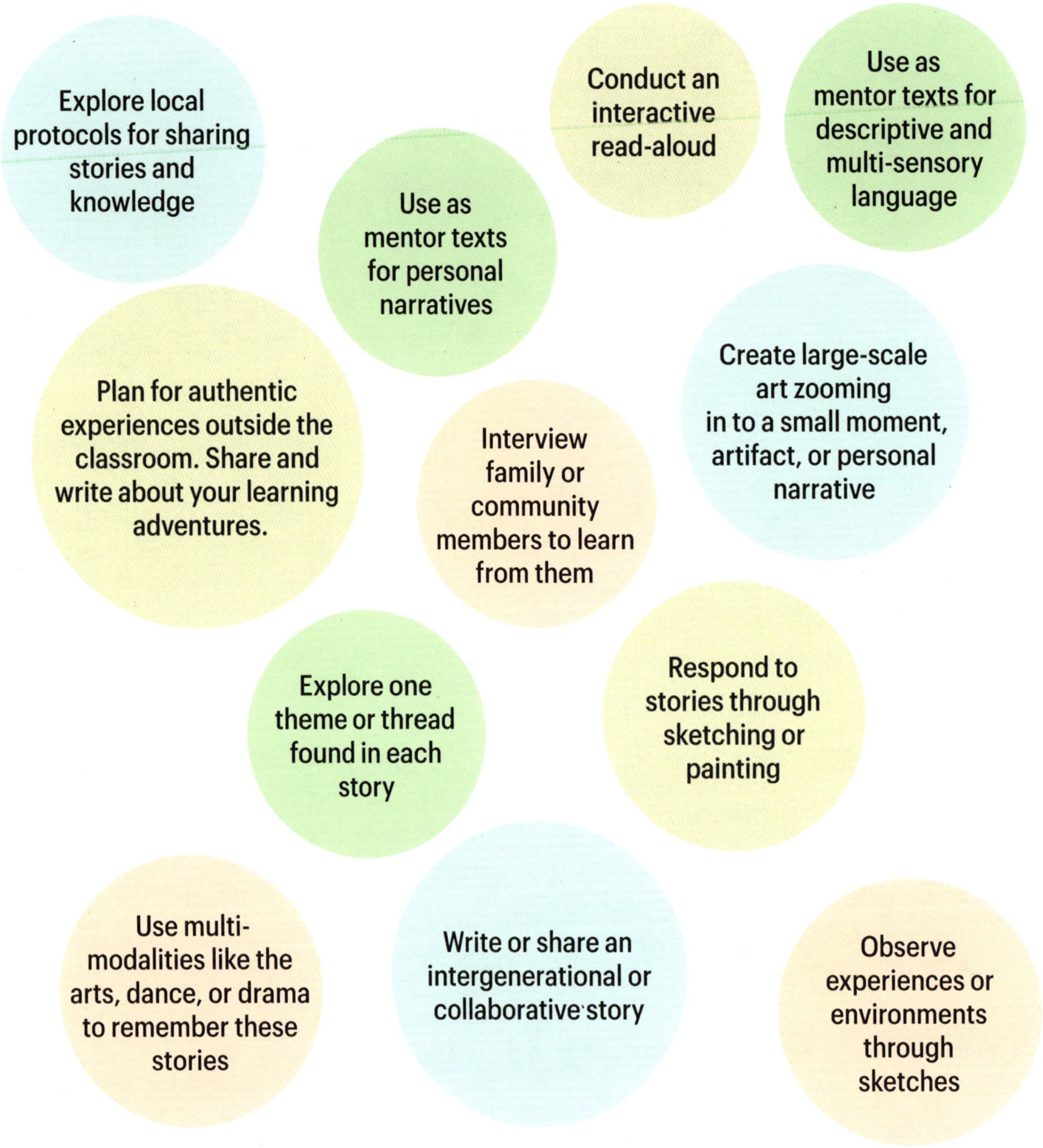

Figure 10. A sampling of Sk̲'ad'a activities

SK̲'AD'A PRINCIPLES IN THE STORIES

Each reader brings their own unique storied lives and experiences to a story. Rather than identifying all Sk̲'ad'a principles found in every book, this chart identifies ones that stand out. Some principles are clearer in the text, some are embedded in the images, and some may emerge over time through the process of sharing.

			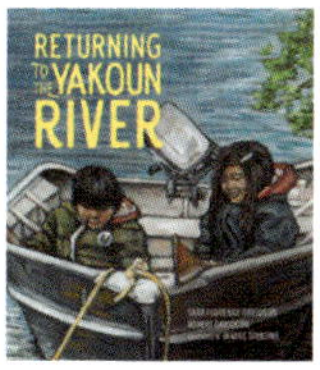	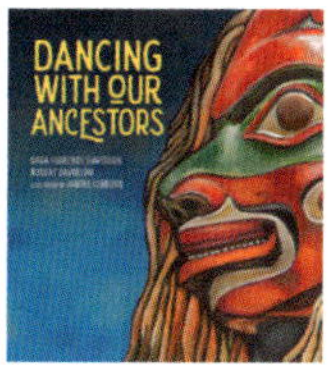
Learning Emerges from **Strong Relationships**	Robert learning from his tsinii	Robert learning from his father and tsinii	Sara and her brother learning from their family	Children and grandchildren learning from and within family and community
Learning Emerges from **Authentic Experiences**	Robert learning while on the boat while fishing	Robert learning while carving	Sara and her brother learning while engaging in the activities	Children learning while dancing
Learning Emerges from **Curiosity**		Robert asking his tsinii questions about carving *Robert being curious about what makes a carving great when learning to carve	*Children learning where to sit on the teeter-totter	*Robert hosting potlatches and feasts because of his own curiosity about them
Learning Occurs through **Observation**	*Robert learning to jig from watching his tsinii	Robert learning from other carvers by copying from old books	Sara's brother (Ben) seeing the sediment in his jug	Sara's uncle teaching children to observe animals to learn how to dance
Learning Occurs through **Contribution**	Tsinii and Robert fishing to share food with family	Robert's dad reminding him to help the family by doing chores	The family expecting children to help with the preparation of the salmon Children going to get water with their tsinii	Community volunteers preparing food and setting the tables

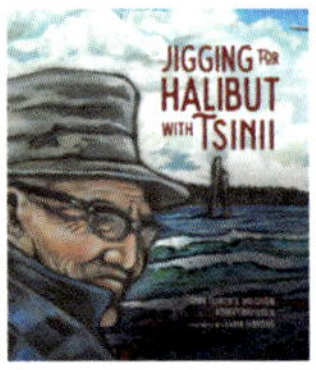

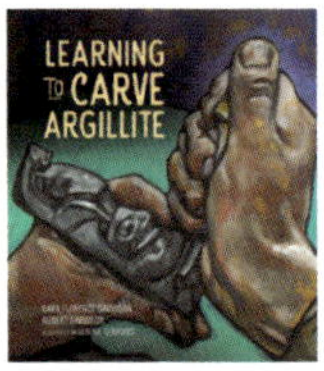

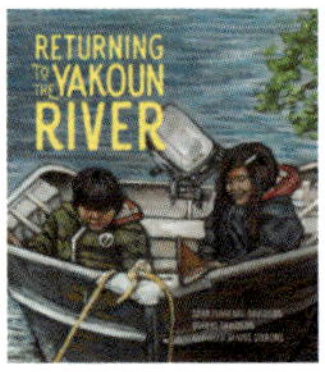

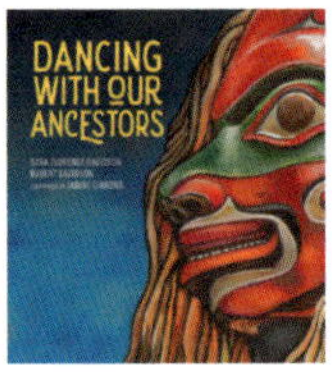

	Jigging for Halibut with Tsinii	Learning to Carve Argillite	Returning to the Yakoun River	Dancing with Our Ancestors
Learning Occurs through **Recognizing and Encouraging Strengths**		*Robert being encouraged to carve by his family		*Dancers being selected to perform specific dances based on their skills with those dances
Learning Honours the **Power of the Mind**	*The practice of preparing the halibut and telling the halibut, "Make your mind strong"			*Indigenous peoples enduring the attempted assimilation and performing dances again
Learning Honours **History and Story**				The sharing of Clan and crest history
Learning Honours **Spirituality and Protocol**	Tsinii speaking to the halibut and rubbing bait on its eyes		Robert returning the salmon bones to the river	Dancers engaging in ceremonial dancing Clans sharing information about crests

*These learning experiences are not explicitly written about in the story. See *Potlatch as Pedagogy: Learning Through Ceremony* for more information about these learning experiences.

  ISBN: 978-1-77492-047-3

BOOK-SPECIFIC SUPPORTS

The following section includes book-specific activities and ideas for engaging with students.

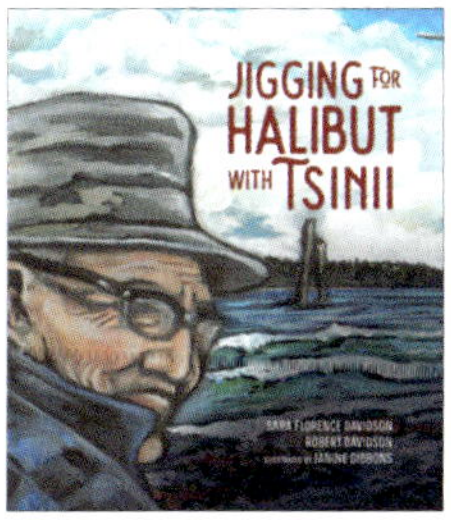

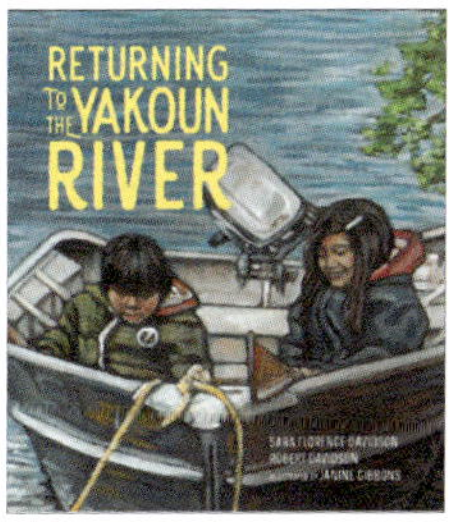

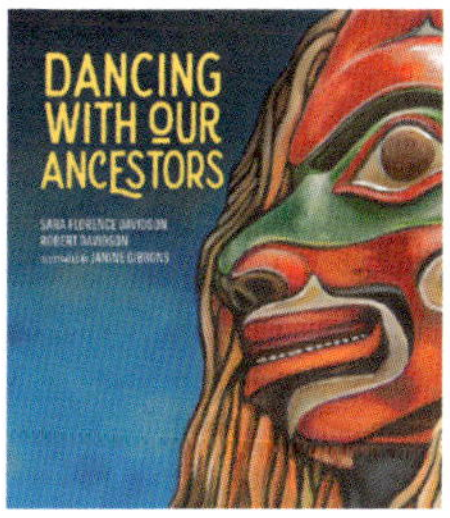

  ISBN: 978-1-77492-047-3

JIGGING FOR HALIBUT WITH TSINII

SUMMARY

Off the northern tip of Haida Gwaii, a boy goes fishing with his tsinii (CHIN-ee), his grandfather. As they watch the weather, jig for halibut, and row with the tides, the boy discovers there's more to learn from Tsinii than how to catch a fish.

KEY VOCABULARY

Sea lice
Halibut
Gaff
Tsinii (CHIN-ee)

Janine took time to research the stories behind every detail of the book—from the fish eye (Figure 8) to the rope knots (Figure 9) to the gaff and club (Figure 11). They are part of her own connection to visual imagery and Haida stories.

Figure 11. Gaff and club
Photo from Janine Gibbons, used with permission

Janine's inspiration for creating the images came from a lived experience. She went out onto the water with a life-size halibut drawing and re-enacted the motions and actions shared in the Davidsons' story. This gave Janine a real sense of how one might move and feel in a small wooden boat on the ocean waves.

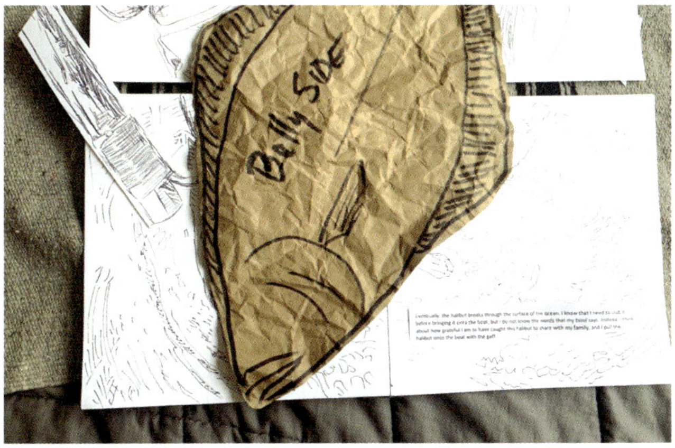

Figure 12. Sketch of in-progress illustrations with life-size halibut drawing that Janine carried with her on the boat and on land to recreate the images
Photo from Janine Gibbons, used with permission

Voice of the Illustrator: Here are a few images of the dinghy that I painted into the story. Tsinii built his own boat and oars, which would have been similar to the Davis boats of Metlakatla, another story that needs to be told. Beautiful boats. Hand-milled wood. The wood expands in the water, so you need to soak the boat, and the cracks then fill in. My neighbour here in Petersburg, Alaska, builds these boats in the identical fashion and allowed me to use the one I painted into the story.

Figure 13. Recreated Davis boat
Photo from Janine Gibbons, used with permission

Figure 14. Sketch of in-progress illustration.
Photo from Janine Gibbons, used with permission

TEACHER GUIDE FOR THE SK̲'AD'A STORIES © 2022 PORTAGE & MAIN PRESS ISBN: 978-1-77492-047-3

INQUIRY WITH STUDENTS: With the class, share Janine's images of the dinghy she painted and her explanation about the Davis boats. Have students investigate further, guided by the questions: Who made Davis boats and what is their story? How are they made? Why are they significant?

RESPONDING WITH THE ARTS

- Share Janine's progress sketch (Figure 15) with students and explain her process. Then have students dramatize a response to the book. Just as Janine did, have students use their bodies to act out catching a halibut. Have them create a tableau to explore the shape and dynamic of being on the boat on the ocean and the movements of their bodies as they jig for halibut.

Figure 15. Sketch of in-progress illustrations and photo of Janine's son, Reid Reucker, helping with the process
Photos from Janine Gibbons, used with permission

  ISBN: 978-1-77492-047-3

REFLECTING

How does Robert learn by "listening to his tsinii in his silence"? When have you listened and learned from someone by their silence?

Voice of the Illustrator: This painting which looks like it could be either ocean or space . . . It is showing the formation of Robert's thought, with the halibut formline emerging from the waves . . . the language of the ocean.

Figure 16. Artwork from Janine Gibbons, used with permission

THINKING CRITICALLY

This story depicts a respectful way of fishing that honours the fish and ensures the sustainability of the fish population. Have students look up reports on current fishing issues in the media, or research different kinds of fishing practices and compare and contrast (e.g., practices that honour versus efficiency).

  ISBN: 978-1-77492-047-3

LEARNING TO CARVE ARGILLITE

SUMMARY

Learning to carve is a lifelong journey. With the help of his father and grandfather, a boy on Haida Gwaii practises to become a skillful carver. As he carefully works on a new piece, he remembers a trip to Slatechuck Mountain to gather the argillite, as well as his father's words about the importance of looking back to help us find our way.

Based on Haida artist Robert Davidson's childhood experiences, this beautiful story highlights learning through observation, as well as the role of Elders in sharing knowledge and mentorship.

KEY VOCABULARY

Argillite (AR-jil-ite)
Gunny sack
Chisels
Gouges

Janine talks about the language of the rocks and how the mountain is speaking, and the artist is listening to what stories, knowledges, and symbols the mountain shares. Janine speaks about the "freeing of argillite." The carvings are more than just material objects with beautiful artistic designs. Janine says, "Symbols are alive and represent supernatural genealogy."

Janine chose to depict sharks on the inside cover of the book (Figure 17) because argillite carvings used to be polished with sand shark skin, which gave them a unique sheen.

Figure 17: Artwork from Janine Gibbons, used with permission

  ISBN: 978-1-77492-047-3

RESEARCHING

Explain that argillite is a rock that comes from Haida Gwaii, specifically Slatechuck Mountain. Have students research argillite to find out more.

REFLECTING

- According to Janine Gibbons, the journey to collect argillite at Slatechuck Mountain is part of the artists' or carvers' process. Carvers have an idea in mind before going on this journey so that they take the appropriate size and shape of argillite.
- Explore texture and properties of argillite by looking at online resources or digital exhibits.

THINKING CRITICALLY

- Argillite carvings are in many museums' collections. Have students seek out articles about how museums have treated, taken, or restored Haida artifacts.
- Explore the significance of using artistic talents to revive culture. What evidence of this do you see in your local/school community? How does art reflect a community's culture? Consider what our world would be like without art. What role does art play in reviving culture?

  ISBN: 978-1-77492-047-3

RETURNING TO THE YAKOUN RIVER

SUMMARY

Based on author Sara Florence Davidson's childhood memories, this illustrated story captures the joy and adventure of a Haida fish camp.

Every spring, a Haida girl and her family travel up the Yakoun River on Haida Gwaii, following the salmon. While their father fishes, the girl and her brother spend their time on the land playing and learning from Tsinii (Grandfather).

RESEARCHING

- Locate the Yakoun River on a map.
- Use live satellite images to get a sense of the land and waters.
- Research connections between the logging industry and the declining sockeye populations.

REFLECTING

"Clocks have no meaning at the river. Instead, we follow the coming and going of the tides." Reflect on this statement.

- Is there something that you do based on the Earth's natural rhythms?
- How did you learn to follow this form of time?

Figure 18: In-progress sketch for *Returning to the Yakoun River*
Artwork from Janine Gibbons, used with permission

  ISBN: 978-1-77492-047-3

Figure 19: In-progress sketch for *Returning to the Yakoun River*
Artwork from Janine Gibbons, used with permission

RESPONDING WITH THE ARTS

- Have students create a tableau in front of a projector to recreate actions from the story, and then trace the images to create large-scale art pieces.
- Have students pick their own personal narrative and write about it. Have them work together to create tableaus that bring their stories to life.

THINKING CRITICALLY

Fishing in the Yakoun River is no longer experienced in the same way as it is described in this book, due to dwindling fish populations. According to Robert Davidson, the sockeye salmon population in the Yakoun River is significantly lower in 2021 than when he was younger. Along with the loss of fish, the stories and potential to pass this authentic experience on to future generations are also lost. When reading with students, address these realities but also encourage them to inquire more into these issues and to take action. How might we become more curious about ongoing issues of sustainability?

DANCING WITH OUR ANCESTORS

SUMMARY

The invitations have been sent. The food has been prepared. The decorations have been hung. And now the day of the potlatch has finally arrived! Guests from all over come to witness this joyful celebration of Haida culture and community. In this tender picture book, Sara Florence Davidson transports readers to the excitement of a potlatch in Hydaburg, Alaska—her last memory of dancing with her late brother.

KEY VOCABULARY

K'aaw (herring roe)
Kawkaahl (leftovers)
Haw'aa (thank you)
Dance screen with crest
Clans

RESEARCHING

For more on the potlatch ban see *Potlatch as Pedagogy*. Be mindful that **Haida potlatches are not to be replicated or recreated in other contexts** as they are ceremonies based on Haida spiritual practices and protocols. Recreating a Haida potlatch in other contexts is cultural appropriation.

REFLECTING

- The Haida potlatch was considered a court of law. What connections can you make between Canadian courts of law and the potlatch? Why do you think the Haida considered the potlatch their court of law?
- Why do you think the government would outlaw the potlatch?
- Does this story remind you of someone in your life who you miss and have fond memories of—someone who is with your ancestors?

RESPONDING WITH THE ARTS

The book highlights the importance of spending time observing the movements and behaviours of animals to know how to become them. Try this as a class. Pick an animal to observe in your local community or research online. Encourage students to embody these movements. How might these animals interact?

  ISBN: 978-1-77492-047-3

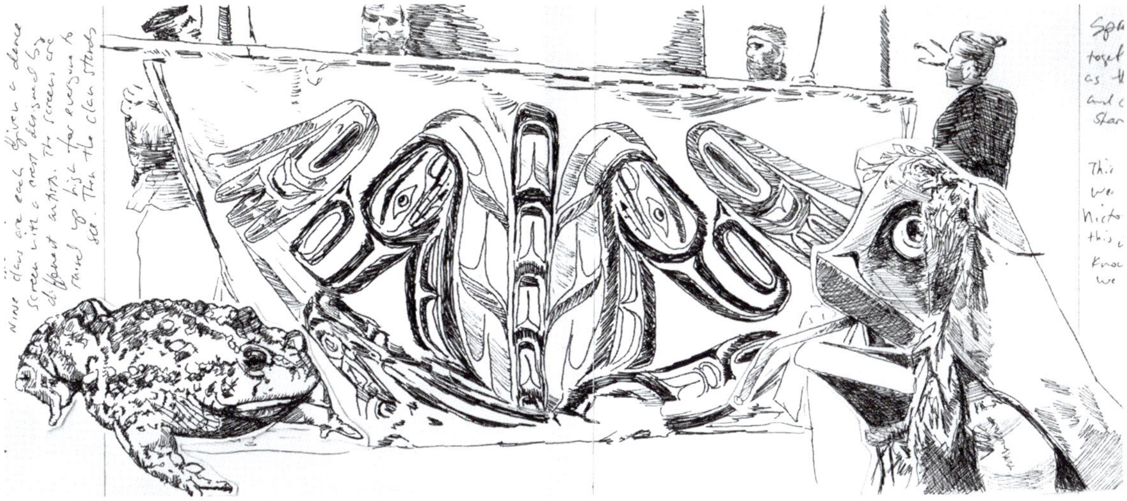

Figure 20: In-progress sketch for *Dancing With Our Ancestors*
Artwork from Janine Gibbons, used with permission

THINKING CRITICALLY

- "... they learn their culture by living it": Have students think of non-textbook examples of lived practices that preserve historical knowledge.
- Discuss the passage that says: "I think about the laws that tried to stop us from gathering, to stop us from singing our songs, to stop us from wearing our regalia, and to stop us from dancing. They wanted us to stop being Haida."
- Reflect on the significance for young members of the Haida Nation of living post-potlatch ban and growing up dancing and singing side by side.

RESOURCES

Clans and Moieties

Sealaska Heritage Institute

The territory of the Haida Nation crosses into what is currently known as Alaska in the United States. This Alaska-based resource provides information about clans and moieties for the Tlingit, Tsimshian, and Haida Nations.

https://www.sealaskaheritage.org/sites/default/files/Unit%207_2.pdf

Council of the Haida Nation

Find information and resources on this website regarding citizenship, land and marine titles, rights, governance, history, languages, and environmental protections.

https://www.haidanation.ca/haida-nation/

Haida Carver

National Film Board of Canada

This 12-minute documentary features Robert Davidson as a young man going to Slatechuck Mountain to choose argillite and features footage of his tsinii, Robert Davidson Sr. It documents the process of carving argillite and provides numerous examples. Note that the language of the voice-over and text do not reflect the most current and appropriate terminology (e.g., "Indians"), and it should be viewed through a critical lens. Consider previewing it and making notes. Then view it with students without the sound, and have stopping points for discussion throughout. The imagery will be helpful.

https://www.nfb.ca/film/haida-carver/

Haida Modern

Knowledge Network

This documentary shares the art and advocacy of Robert Davidson.

https://www.knowledge.ca/program/haida-modern (Note: Requires a free account).

Potlatch as Pedagogy: Learning Through Ceremony

Sara Florence Davidson and Robert Davidson

This book includes background and contextual information for a better understanding of the historical and cultural significance of the Sk̲'ad'a Stories. It also supports a deeper understanding of Haida ceremony and protocols, while providing information about the threats to culture imposed by the Canadian government.

Raven Calling Productions

This website includes helpful information including songs, albums, language links, and contemporary Haida art exhibits by Haida artist, lawyer, and activist Gid7ahl-G̲udsllaay Lalaxaaygans Terri-Lynn Williams-Davidson. This site also includes materials to support *Magical Beings of Haida Gwaii*, a children's book co-written by Gid7ahl-G̲udsllaay Lalaxaaygans Terri-Lynn Williams-Davidson and Sara Florence Davidson.

https://www.ravencallingproductions.ca

  ISBN: 978-1-77492-047-3

Returning the Past: Repatriation of First Nations Cultural Property

Museum of Anthropology at the University of British Columbia

Consult this unit of study for secondary school students to learn about some of the issues regarding the repatriation of cultural artifacts.

https://moa.ubc.ca/wp-content/uploads/2014/09/School_TeacherAid-RepatriationCaseStudies.pdf

Sara Florence Davidson's blog

This blog provides a reflection of Sara's research and publications and public responses, such as "Raising the Issues with the 'Family Totem Pole.'" Learn more about Sara Florence Davidson and her ongoing work with this collection.

http://saraflorence.ca/blog/

Teacher

BC Teacher's Federation magazine

See page 22 of the May/June 2020 issue for the article "Evaluating Indigenous Education Resources for Classroom Use" by Sara Florence Davidson. Sara presents questions to consider when evaluating and selecting Indigenous education resources.

https://www.bctf.ca/docs/default-source/publications/publications-teacher-magazine/teacher-may-2020.pdf?sfvrsn=66291b19_0

REFERENCES

Archibald, J. (n.d.). *On becoming story-ready* [Video]. Indigenous storywork. https://indigenousstorywork.com/1-for-educators/

Archibald, J. (2008). *Indigenous storywork: Educating the heart, mind, body, and spirit.* UBC Press.

Archibald, J. (2020). Finding the bone needle through Indigenous storywork. In E. S. Huaman & N. D. Martin (Eds.), *Indigenous knowledge systems and research methodologies: Local solutions and global opportunities* (pp. 18–35). Canadian Scholars.

Baird, J. R., Solanki, A., & Askren, M. (2008). *Returning the past: Repatriation of First Nations cultural property.* UBC Museum of Anthropology. https://moa.ubc.ca/wp-content/uploads/2014/09/School_TeacherAid-RepatriationCaseStudies.pdf

British Columbia. (2021). Haida Gwaii. In *BC Geographical Names.* https://apps.gov.bc.ca/pub/bcgnws/names/61561.html

Council of the Haida Nation (2021). *History of the Haida Nation.* https://www.haidanation.ca/haida-nation/

Davidson, R., & Davidson, S. F. (2016). Make your mind strong: My father's insights into academic success. *Canadian Journal of Education, 39*(2). https://journals.sfu.ca/cje/index.php/cje-rce/article/view/2139/1843

Davidson, R, & Davidson, S. F. (2018) *Potlatch as pedagogy: Learning through ceremony.* Portage & Main Press.

Davidson, S. F. (2020, May/June). Evaluating Indigenous education resources for classroom use. *Teacher Magazine* [Publication of BC Teacher's Federation], *32*(5), pp. 22–23. https://www.bctf.ca/docs/default-source/publications/publications-teacher-magazine/teacher-may-2020.pdf?sfvrsn=66291b19_0

Gordon, E., & Archibald, J. (1994). Storyguide: Beginning the journey. In A. Goodfellow, *First Nations journeys of justice: Building bridges of understanding between nations (Grade Three)* (pp. 35–58). Law Courts Education Society of British Columbia.

Haiken, Melanie (2020, February 3). *Visiting Haida Gwaii, Canada's most mysterious islands.* CNN. https://www.cnn.com/travel/article/haida-gwaii-canada-islands/index.html

McIntosh, E. (2020, January 24). What we mean when we say Indigenous land is "unceded." *Canada's National Observer.* https://www.nationalobserver.com/2020/01/24/analysis/what-we-mean-when-we-say-indigenous-land-unceded

National Council of Teachers of English. (2021). *Catching the bug for reading through interactive read-alouds.* ReadWriteThink. https://www.readwritethink.org/classroom-resources/lesson-plans/catching-reading-through-interactive

Pahl, K., & Roswell, J. (2010). *Artifactual literacies: Every object tells a story.* Teachers College Press.

Truth and Reconciliation Commission of Canada [TRC]. (2015). *The final report of the Truth and Reconciliation Commission of Canada: Vol. 6. Canada's residential schools: Reconciliation.* McGill-Queen's University Press.

Tuck, E., & Gaztambide-Fernández, R. A. (2013). Curriculum, replacement, and settler futurity. *JCT Online, 29*(1), pp. 72–89. https://journal.jctonline.org/index.php/jct/article/view/411

Williams-Davidson, Terri-Lynn Gid7ahl-G̲udsllaay Lalaxaaygans. (2017). *Out of concealment: Female supernatural beings of Haida Gwaii.* Heritage House.

  ISBN: 978-1-77492-047-3